PowerKids Readers:

The Bilingual Library of the United States of America™

NEBRASKA

DEAN GALIANO

TRADUCCIÓN AL ESPAÑOL: MARÍA CRISTINA BRUSCA

The Rosen Publishing Group's
PowerKids Press™ & **Editorial Buenas Letras**™
New York

Published in 2006 by The Rosen Publishing Group, Inc.
29 East 21st Street, New York, NY 10010

First Edition

Book Design: Dean Galiano

Photo Credits: Cover © Macduff Everton/Corbis; p. 5 © 2001 One Mile Up, Inc; p. 9 © Tom Bean/Corbis; p. 11 © Francis G. Mayer/Corbis; p. 13 © Bettmann/Corbis; p. 15 © Corbis; p. 17 © Corbis; p. 19 (left) © David Muench/Corbis; p. 19 (middle) © Associated Press, AP; p. 19 (right) © Royalty-free/Corbis; p. 21 © Reuters/Corbis; p. 23 © Royalty-free/Corbis; p. 25 © Annie Griffiths Belt/Corbis; p. 26 © Layne Kennedy/Corbis; p. 30 (capital) © Philip Gould/Corbis; p. 30 (seal) © 2001 One Mile Up, Inc; p. 30 (flower) © Gunter Marx/Corbis; p. 30 (bird) © Darrel Gulin/Corbis; p. 30 (tree) © W. Perry Conway/Corbis; p. 30 (agate) © M. Angelo/Corbis; p. 31 (upper left) © Bettmann/Corbis; p. 31 (upper middle) © Bettmann/Corbis; p. 31 (upper right) © Bettmann/Corbis; p. 31 (lower left) © Bettmann/Corbis; p. 31. (lower middle) © Bettmann/Corbis; p. 31 (lower right) © Wyman Ira/Corbis Sygma

Library of Congress Cataloging-in-Publication Data

Galiano, Dean.
Nebraska / Dean Galiano ; traducción al español, María Cristina Brusca. —1st ed.
p. cm. — (Bilingual library of the United States of America) English and Spanish.
Includes bibliographical references and index.
ISBN 1-4042-3092-0 (library binding)
1. Nebraska—Juvenile literature. I. Title. II. Series.
F666.3.G35 2006
978.2—dc22
2005013787

Manufactured in the United States of America

Due to the changing nature of Internet links, Editorial Buenas Letras has developed an online list of Web sites related to the subject of this book. This site is updated regularly. Please use this link to access the list:

http://www.buenasletraslinks.com/ls/nebraska

Contents

Contenido

Welcome to Nebraska

Nebraska became the thirty-seventh state in 1867. The state seal shows a banner with the state motto, "Equality Before the Law." The motto reminds us that all the people in Nebraska have the same rights.

Bienvenidos a Nebraska

Nebraska se convirtió en el estado treinta y siete en el año 1867. El escudo muestra una banda con el lema del estado, "Igualdad ante la ley". Este lema nos recuerda que todas las personas en Nebraska tienen los mismos derechos.

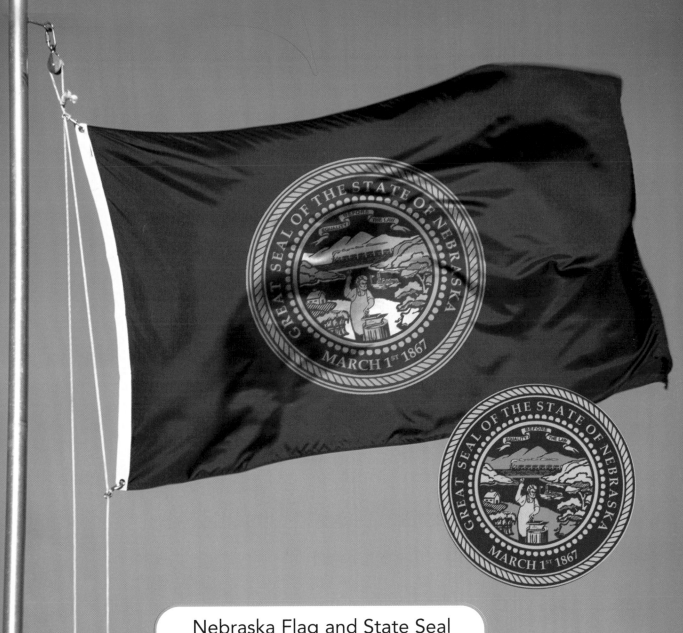

Nebraska Flag and State Seal

Bandera y escudo de Nebraska

Nebraska Geography

Nebraska is located in the central United States. Nebraska borders the states of South Dakota, Iowa, Missouri, Kansas, Colorado, and Wyoming.

Geografía de Nebraska

Nebraska está situado en la región central de los Estados Unidos. Nebraska linda con los estados de Dakota del Sur, Iowa, Misuri, Kansas, Colorado y Wyoming.

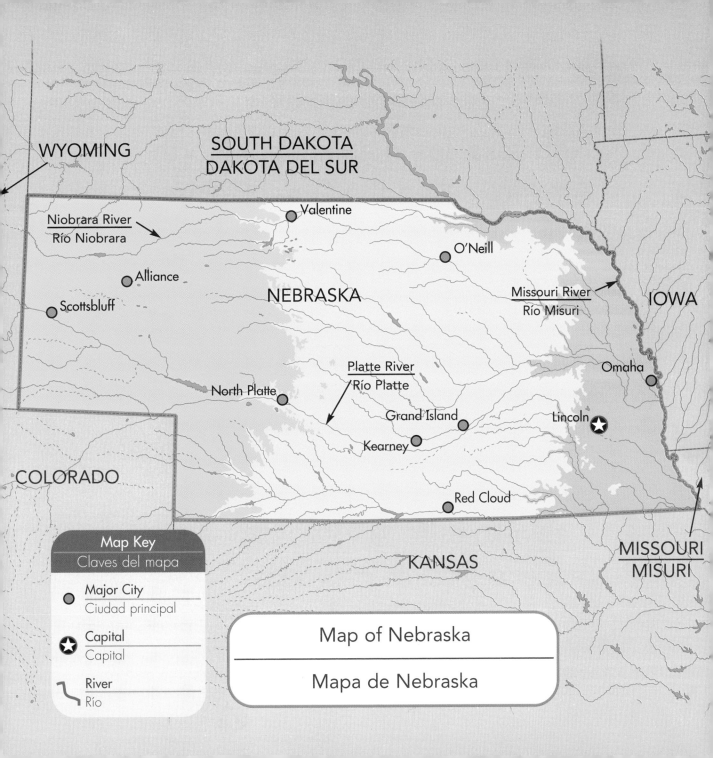

WYOMING

SOUTH DAKOTA
DAKOTA DEL SUR

Niobrara River
Río Niobrara

Valentine

O'Neill

Alliance

Scottsbluff

NEBRASKA

Missouri River
Río Misuri

IOWA

Platte River
Río Platte

North Platte

Grand Island

Omaha

Lincoln

Kearney

COLORADO

Red Cloud

KANSAS

MISSOURI
MISURI

Map Key
Claves del mapa

Major City
Ciudad principal

Capital
Capital

River
Río

Map of Nebraska

Mapa de Nebraska

Nebraska lies in an area of North America called the Great Plains. Most of Nebraska is flat and is covered by farmland or grassland.

Nebraska se encuentra en una región de Norteamérica llamada las Grandes Llanuras. La mayoría del suelo de Nebraska es llano y está cubierto de praderas y tierras cultivadas.

Ogallala National Grassland

Pradera Nacional Oglala

Nebraska History

In the 1800s, Nebraska was populated mostly by Native Americans. The Native American tribes farmed and hunted for their food.

Historia de Nebraska

En 1854, Nebraska estaba poblada en su mayoría por nativos americanos. Las tribus nativoamericanas cultivaban la tierra y cazaban para obtener sus alimentos.

Native Americans Hunting for Buffalo

Nativos americanos en una cacería de búfalo

Chief Red Cloud was born in Nebraska in 1822. In 1866, he fought a war against the U.S. Army. Red Cloud spent his life fighting for the rights of Native Americans.

El jefe Red Cloud nació en Nebraska en 1822. Red Cloud significa "Nube Roja". En 1866, Red Cloud lideró una guerra en contra del ejército de E.U.A. Durante toda su vida, Red Cloud luchó por los derechos de los nativos americanos.

Red Cloud, 1822–1909

Red Cloud (1822–1909)

Nebraska became a state in 1867. The first railroad was built across the state in the same year. The railroad brought a large number of settlers to Nebraska.

Nebraska llegó a ser un estado en 1867. Ese mismo año fue construído el primer ferrocarril a través del estado. El ferrocarril atrajo muchos colonos a Nebraska.

The Omaha Railroad Depot in Eastern Nebraska

Despacho del Ferrocarril Omaha en Nebraska oriental

In 1862, Congress passed the Homestead Act. This act gave free land to settlers willing to move west and become farmers. Settlers built homes of mud and plowed the land to plant crops.

En 1862, el congreso aprobó la Ley de Colonización. Esta ley les otorgaba tierras gratuitas a los colonos que desearan ir a vivir al oeste para ser granjeros. Los colonos construyeron viviendas de barro y cultivaron la tierra.

Settlers near Coburgh, Nebraska, in 1887

Colonos cerca de Coburgh, Nebraska, en 1887

Living in Nebraska

Nebraska is a large state. It is more than 450 miles (724 km) wide. One road called Interstate 80 runs across the state. Many people use the interstate to get from place to place in Nebraska.

La vida en Nebraska

Nebraska es un estado muy grande. Tiene más de 450 millas (724 km) de ancho. Una ruta, llamada Interestatal 80, atraviesa el estado. Mucha gente utiliza esta ruta interestatal para viajar de un lugar a otro de Nebraska.

Courthouse Rock, Oregon Trail Landmark
Courthouse Rock, sitio histórico de la ruta de Oregón

Grain Storage in Tamora
Silos de cereales en Tamora

Skyline of Downtown Omaha
Vista del centro de Omaha

Kimball

Ogallala

North Platte

Grand Island

Kearney

Lincoln

Omaha

Map Key
Claves del mapa

- **Major City**
  Ciudad principal

- **Capital**
  Capital

- **Interstate 80**
  Ruta Interestatal 80

Interstate 80

Ruta Interestatal 80

Many Nebraskans enjoy football. Their football team is called the Cornhuskers. People watch the Cornhuskers play on Saturdays in the fall.

Muchos nebrasqueños disfrutan del fútbol americano. Su equipo favorito se llama Cornhuskers. La gente asiste a los partidos de los Cornhuskers, los sábados, durante la temporada de otoño

The Cornhuskers of Nebraska University

Los Cornhuskers de la Universidad de Nebraska

Nebraska Today

Nearly two million people call Nebraska home. Omaha is the largest city in the state. Omaha is home to many important businesses.

Nebraska, hoy

Casi dos millones de personas viven en Nebraska. Omaha es la ciudad más grande del estado. Omaha es la sede de muchas empresas importantes.

Omaha Skyline

Vista de Omaha

Ashfall Fossil Beds State Park opened in 1991. Many animal fossils have been discovered at Ashfall. Some of them are more than 10 million years old!

El Parque Estatal Ashfall Fossil Beds se inauguró en 1991. Muchos fósiles animales han sido descubiertos en Ashfall. ¡Algunos de ellos tienen más de 10 millones de años de antigüedad!

Ten-Million-Year-Old Rhinoceros found in Ashfall

Rinoceronte de diez millones de años encontrado en Ashfall

Activity:
Let's Draw Chimney Rock
Chimney Rock is a famous landmark
along the Oregon Trail.

Actividad:
Dibujemos Chimney Rock
Chimney Rock es un famoso sitio histórico de la Ruta de Oregón

1

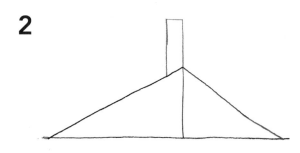

Draw two triangles that share
one line as shown.

Dibuja dos triángulos que
compartan una línea, como se
ve en el ejemplo.

2

Draw the shape on the top of
the first triangle.

Dibuja una forma en la parte
superior del primer triángulo.

3

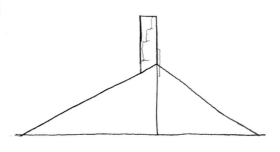

Add lines to form the pointed edges and the bumpy surface of the rock.

Agrega líneas para dar forma a los bordes agudos y a los bultos de la superficie de la roca.

4

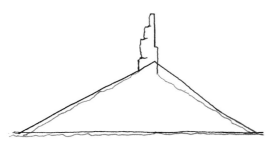

Erase extra lines. Draw wavy lines along the edges of the triangles.

Borra las líneas innecesarias. Dibuja líneas onduladas sobre los bordes de los triángulos.

5

Erase all extra lines. Add shading and detail to your drawing.

Borra todas las líneas sobrantes. Agrega sombras y detalles a tu dibujo.

Timeline		Cronología
Frenchman Étienne Veniard de Bourgmont is the first European to journey to Nebraska.	**1714**	El francés Étienne Veniard de Bourgmont es el primer europeo en viajar a Nebraska.
The United States buys the area of Nebraska in the Louisiana Purchase.	**1803**	Los Estados Unidos compran la región de Nebraska en la Compra de Luisiana.
Fort Kearny is built along the Oregon Trail.	**1848**	Se construye el Fuerte Kearny sobre la Ruta de Oregón.
Congress passes the Homestead Act and the Pacific Railroad Act.	**1862**	La Ley de Colonización y la del Ferrocarril del Pacífico son aprobadas en el congreso.
Nebraska becomes the thirty-seventh state.	**1867**	Nebraska se convierte en el estado treinta y siete.
Robert Anderson is the first black person to homestead in Nebraska.	**1870**	Robert Anderson, primer colono negro del estado, se establece en Nebraska.
Gerald Ford of Omaha becomes president of the United States.	**1974**	Gerald Ford, nativo de Omaha, llega a ser presidente de los Estados Unidos.

Nebraska Events	Eventos en Nebraska
February Nebraska Cattlemen's Classic in Kearney	Febrero Clásico de ganaderos, en Kearny
February to Late March Sandhill Crane Spring Migration along Platte River valley	Febrero hasta fines de marzo Migración de primavera de la grulla Sandhill, a lo largo del valle del río Platte
March St. Patrick's Day Celebration in O'Neill	Marzo Celebraciones del Día de San Patricio, en O'Neill
April Willa Cather Spring Festival in Red Cloud	Abril Festival de primavera Willa Cather, en Red Cloud
May Nebraska Renaissance Fair in Omaha	Mayo Feria renacimiento de Nebraska
June College World Series in Omaha Cottonwood Festival in Hastings	Junio Serie mundial universitaria, en Omaha Festival del álamo, en Hastings
August and Early September Nebraska State Fair in Lincoln	Agosto hasta principios de Septiembre Feria del estado de Nebraska, en Lincoln
September River City Roundup in Omaha	Septiembre Arreo River City, en Omaha

Nebraska Facts/Datos sobre Nebraska

Population
1.7 million

Población
1.7 millones

Capital
Lincoln

Capital
Lincoln

State Motto
Equality Before the Law

Lema del estado
Igualdad ante la ley

State Flower
Goldenrod

Flor del estado
Vara de oro

State Bird
Western Meadowlark

Ave del estado
Pradero occidental

State Nickname
The Cornhusker State

Mote del estado
Estado Cornhusker
(desgranador de maíz)

State Tree
Cottonwood

Árbol del estado
Álamo

State Song
"Beautiful Nebraska"

Canción del estado
"Hermosa Nebraska"

State Gemstone
Blue Agate

Piedra preciosa
Ágata azul

Famous Nebraskans/Nebrasqueños famosos

Red Cloud
(1822–1909)

Lakota leader
Líder Lakota

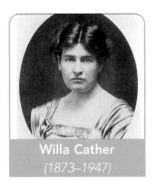

Willa Cather
(1873–1947)

Author
Escritora

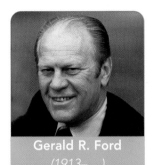

Gerald R. Ford
(1913–   )

U.S. president
Presidente de E.U.A.

Johnny Carson
(1925–2005)

Entertainer
Comediante

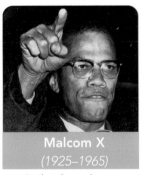

Malcom X
(1925–1965)

Civil rights advocate
Defensor de los derechos civiles

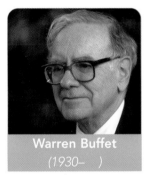

Warren Buffet
(1930–   )

Entrepreneur
Empresario

Words to Know/Palabras que debes saber

fossil
fósil

prairie
pradera

railroad
ferrocarril

settlers
colonos

31

Here are more books to read about Nebraska:
Otros libros que puedes leer sobre Nebraska:

In English/En inglés:

Nebraska
From Sea to Shining Sea
by Weatherly, Myra S.
Children's Press, 2003

Nebraska
Hello U.S.A.
by Porter, A. P.
Lerner Publications, 2002

Words in English: 298

Palabras en español: 315

Index

Índice